Eclectia

J.P. Goss

Note from the author!

First off, I'd like to thank you, the reader, for picking up a copy of my poetry. This being the first output in my oeuvre, it comes with great anxiety to release it into the world; I imagine that those whirlies and their parent trees may feel a similar anxiety.

Regardless, I sincerely hope you enjoy these poems, they are some of the best, in my opinion, of the eclectic, confessional ramblings of a young soul. Hence the name. The name however, came out of a vacuum, or rather in the void of its previous name. Initially, it was to be called "the Adolescent Manifesto," considering much of the subject material totes a feeling of that confusing and painful tumult of youth that everyone goes through, where every day is a struggle for self-definition and in a world of increasing pressures that becomes so much harder to achieve or even legitimize. Yet, an apology of young people may not be the best treatise to impress the entertainment world with, at least to start out.

I settled on "Eclectia" after much thought: perhaps these poems are too all-over-the-place to ascribe a definite theme to them but the postmodern absence of theme: why have to deal with accusations of pretense when I can merely give it honestly? And so I settled on "Eclectia."

I feel, if we can find that one thing that allows us to

comfortably across the world, that thing that we can never let go of, all things will come in time. We may search our whole lives and find nothing satisfying; this is where we must look honestly not simply at ourselves but at perhaps at what is not there in the order. There may be negation, there may be a lack of solidity, but that does not mean that all is empty. There are deeper metaphysical implications that branch from that, but I am not going to discuss them here.

This is the reason, also, why I choose to stylize "Eclectia" with unconventionally positioned E and A. In first-order logic, the E is the existential quantifier, while the

A is the universal; "there exists at least one," "everything that exists is," respectively. There exists at least one thing, even if it is chaotic and senseless, that begins and in its turn becomes everything.

These poems do not speak, per se, a constant theme but they constitute a work that, I hope, bespeaks the spirit of the eclectic: the reorganization of chaos into something beautiful, something empowering, something truly reflecting the soul. Also, these poems are not what you might consider "creative," "innovative," or "fresh." This is the very of eclectic: to make something of several broken things, to reorganize into a way that is, by its very nature,

creative, I invite you as the
reader to make what you can of
these poems; sit and consider
what they mean to you, as with
everything you read; see the
apparent message, but your
intuitions should be the final
judge.

I hope you enjoy it.
--J.P. Goss
1st ed.

Of Solace and Solstice

A road, I will walk
Of rimed old men and invisible
children
A barren 'scape, all uniform and
erudite
A scene to some, so meaningless
and sullen,
But to me, I crave such to behold
a virgin white.
Corrupt, it is not, despite my
trek.
At Peace, my soul, at rest.
Baptize this ailing body, come
the advent of night.

The case of him lacking

A man I knew once
Of nobility and pitiless prose
Forked tongue, a mind who blunted
those of ferrous wits
A soul nurtured by the forest ewe
Adverting stimuli, in solemnity
he sits
A flicker of passion in his
throat arose
Promptly licked by that silent
promise
Condemned to obscurity, like firm
soil he is composed
Ardent and sullen like any
cracked timber,
He remains fixed, as the dead in
peaceful slumber.
All and none, brothers of the
pupil akin
The zenith of event, he has
already been there

Visions of splendor, grandiose
pulchritude, and ruin
Of his that mine eyes seek do not
they dare
Of mine his eyes have never been
so cursed
Blank but fruitful what glory he
has seen
Of things beyond all mortal
belief is he so well versed
Encased in lye and pewter flesh,
No hands were laid upon that
sconce
Preserved in virgin garment,
immune to life's thresh
Did not he ignore a man, but
rather lack response?
Him lacking had no name, but the
case of which him befell
I called, 'tis true, beckoned him
here
And not a nod in my direction

Yet to beseech a brook at the
chine of a knell
A thoughtless benediction
But deluded I, spent drunk
immersion in this life
Drowned by rushing torrents and
temporal maelstrom a reward of
prolix strife
My thoughts composed of endless
lies, theories countless deeds of
fitful right and wrong
Yet he, so pure, have thought
nothing like myself, no speech to
taint his canvas
Nay, he's different, of this I'm
sure
He's not diseased, he's not
impure
For it is I, of adamant ardour,
Who should seek his mindful cure.

In the Grass beneath the trees

There he stood
A shadow cast in the light of
ease
There she sat
In the grass beneath the
blossom'd trees
Perfect world, Perfect mind
All ensconced in his mental
treatise
Enlivened youth, flaring in
cheerful environs
Luminous embrace and Aeolian
minute
Yet she fixed in the shade of
ignorance
Yet he a shade his mind beget
Organs stolid like rock, her
blood afforded such recompense

Watched, did he, the earth wither
in snow
And her fugacious radiance
diminished along the ridge
Great fissures crept, waiting,
without hope to know
For her to return to the trees
To imbue, again, life and dying
to cease
Husk to dust, a forgotten relic
A memory so surreal
Ethereal
Gone with time, gone with breeze
Even the grass
Even the trees
Life a perpetual memento
The finitude of engagement
Her breath, constantly in the air
And he, like the earth
Love and memory, never there.

Houses

There, in a rustic grove behind
the hills
On trails upon which we once
drove
Stood an old house
Nostalgia abounds, my heart it
fills
The timbers creak and glass all
but gone
Strong, loving walls effaced with
time's neglect
Not an eye to peer on its bones
pall
But I remember
Nearest the central pole
The dear mother I did extol
The father I scorned
A body forlorn
The hands veined and vain
The spine slowly receding

The lungs given way, many years
prior
The house is weak the house is
saddened
The house condemned this house is
conceited
Held in time's suspend
Until it is dust
Doomed to compromise in one
telling gust
This house had love this house
was sick
This house left for a time and
left with a mourning shove
It is but a tomb, now
Weathered and rotten with nothing
to show
But the damage sustained
All its appendages
Broken, beaten, cynical
With indifferent blow

The pain of passing is its to
know
The house is shaking
The house, it trembles
The house is deteriorating
I can feel it now
I'll stand by you
As you collapse about me
And timbers split my skull
For my bones shatter too
Flesh vulnerable to the lashes
And pitiless fangs do maim
I'll stay to the end, house,
withal
Entomb at your side
No wind deterred
Nor levy to daunt the rains
And our battle one in the same.

A thought or Two

While the opaque pinks and blues
of the twilight slowly recede to
black
Belief in the goodness of man
Fleeting, a closing act
We war for land that is not ours
Deny our brethren with our towers
Support those who only take
And imbibe for a thirst doomed
never to slake
Don a badge of polarity
Harbor ethics sans consistency
and sincerity
Complacent, ignorant, distracted
Credence to the man by the lake,
we're fools
Willful imprisonment forever
enacted
We truly are the "tools of our
tools."

Our invisible hands our wings
have clipped
Turning ambition to tinder,
action to slumber
A maze to lose us, choked by the
flanks
Our journey constructs
Plank by plank.
Never a more majestic sight,
Enclosure
Painted with hues of human might
erasure
The cracks, the faults become
comfort
Endless channels of flesh become
water
Misery become food
All this welcomed with open arms
Convinced of condemnation,
sufficed with mediocrity
Stagnate do we in our pool
Because it is ultimate beauty

The smog begets a perfect world
How liberating to venture into
unknown unfurled
Without invisible hands
Without the vices of this culture
Without the blackened hearts of
these lands
But with all freedom we crave for
sure
Wait, we don't want what freedom
demands
We love the hands
We love the vices
But opine in heated fits
Within our cages just like happy
little hypocrites
Beasts walking about
With coils tired fast to our skin
Hating those who yank
Yet life beyond is that of sin.

Anomie

So this is what they call anomie?

A grayness,

A blank,

All things devoid of beauty?

When the eternal arms,

Have left me to my own devices,

To toil in deaden land

To paint futile pictures?

I'm wading through waves, through
fires

Surely to send some men to fits,
quite deliriously

And as though it never came to
pass

I sip unsweetened tea.

What rips men apart,

What fetters pull him in twain,

Simply move me with sway

And don't move me at all.

Tears rush like the flume

Admonishments thrown

And I can only sigh in
frustration
At all this petty emotion.
For man fills his stage with
characters,
And bleeds ink all within his
works
Aspiring to his own audience, the
god he is,
I simply abuse this alchemy
To bide my time till death.
Call meaning what you will,
Fill your life with love,
Fill your life with gold,
with God,
with spite,
with studies,
yourself.
I cannot,
I do not,
I know not these simple pleasures
Perpetually I am not full,

For there exists where faith
should be
A deep impartial hole
If I could be normal,
If I could love or only believe,
I'd turn away from it,
And choose to stare uselessly
into my faithless hole,
All things beat on, as they be,
And this conviction, be it ever
so keen,
That existence and living are
useless things,
I'd still see what believers
still see
That being the world as beauty,
I'd only see it with a more
grayish hue
(Without the pretension to know
what is true!)
And see the sense it lacks to see
And commit myself to this anomie.

Happy One

Look there, Happy One
The rain beats on and thunder
crack
Long since sky was swallowed
A tempest arises to batter the
elms
The maelstrom duly followed.
The howl is rending, my sanity
spent
While taunted all alone,
I fear this echoes of days of
lore
I speak of divine punishment
The sky wails with its torment
And confines me to a cell
Where screams as loud as grinding
stones
Inculcate my little hell.
More and more they flee the storm
Running to the depths
For they delude themselves upon

Outrunning life upon their steps.

Walls do darken as day dies away

Born to rise and die as youth

Younger and younger

While fighting, scarring,

cracking skin and tooth.

Yet here I stand to give my piece

With mark of spear on wrist and

chest

Take the chalice of storm and

life

And drink its flooding water

The unity is bless'd.

Still I hope and carry on

Tarrying too long

Flirting with the gilded chance

That does me so much wrong.

Why do I flagellate

Happy One, hasten tell

Why is your happy, brilliant

world

Forsaken, bleak, and fell?

Not all is lost, I hear you all
proclaim
Misery has it foil
That love is precious and abounds
With little work and toil
Yet I say to you
The very shoots from Love is
pluck'd
Are sowed in soil, firm and fully
parched
Nourish'd by desire
Where before my eyes, awe struck
Are acid pools and mire.
Beyond that Love just tastes of
piss
Despite its outward candoris
Our fleshy evils we find just
Ignoring that our Love is Lust.
Where then, Happy One
Do I find respite?
Where is this sacred mystery
That's optimistic trite?

You lie, you know,

Its tendrils fling 'cross Chronos

and the Gaia

As huge as our importance

As impregnable as the taiga.

The sky has darken'd like a

corpse

The night with but a duller moon

The Happy One has run away

His world I have hewn.

They all have stopped running

The rain ceases to be

And here they chant and shout and

scream

"We've outrun the dreaded rain,

Saved ourselves!" collectively.

Day has died, and so have we,

Yet, make the best

In this wakened state

The staring at the coffin lid,

For each morn, I do recall

Every dewy, lambent infancy

Imbibing life into us all
Though so bright come noon time
Began, wan, birthed it was to
pall.
So speak, Happy One
Tell me I'm among you
Tell me I'm disposed to running
from the night
That cynically I'll sate myself
Decrying it a human blight
Yet I can't find the mettle
Within my own flawed skin
To kill a feeling so close to me
To slaughter my own kin
Iron hits the ground again
In hated acceptance, pure
dejection
I can't explain the darkest truth
Commandeering the realm of ken
With both illusions, Hope and
Love
In plain, unaltered sight

Embittered me will wail out loud
To you, oh Happy One
That we were always right.

The Ides have kept me thus far

These ides have kept me thus far
Sustained, am I, eternal
By their food of self-sacrifice
The jester's tasty wine
Imbibing insults wrought by
fool'ry
Again, reciting the dirge for
pride
But the ides have kept me thus
far.
Despite the ru'nation
Hoist! Ye ru'nous hands
That old way in mortification
A fool by their and my demands
I see my shame, long shadow cast
In light of sobriety
Ignominy and truth of me
Divorc'd n'er they be

Still taste of cheap liquors,
distilled society
But the ides have kept me thus
far.
Full knowledge, have I
The disservice I do
Only time will heal the wound
To shy away, acceptance is
A lovely balm on par
My image in tatters, though
brazen I be
The ides have kept me thus far
Let them laugh, for I know they
do
Not to me, but within and among
I am your entertainment
The source of all your jeers
My life, a blund'ring show
I am an actor, my blight for
years
A part to play, it's pleasing
though

To thrive upon your mocking and
time
Comforting knowledge, that
A fixture, am I, your Thalia
The ides have kept me thus far
Erected austerity, enigmatic
walls
Fortifications around me
Charged to keep the chaos in
My heart, it truly calls
I am not so noble
As the sun will attest
Know me as the ascetic,
See the shrieking eccentric,
Know me as the philosopher
See my wit pathetic,
Know what is outside is purely
for show
See that is internalized, is
So goddamned antithetic
Each and every time
I hide my face in shame

My pride and my name, my actions
did thus mar
But I will heal, I always do
The ides have kept me thus far
This is my mantra, an empty
cadence
A mist to latch on to
With every refrain of wretched
debauchery
Each weekend played anew
Though I stay to bear the howl
Of my dissonant, ugly hymn
I listen to the hardened ones
Their failures but a din
I wish to change the thing I am
At least to those who know
I've heaved the chance to the icy
mar
Onto the cracking floe
I feel the daggers of humiliation
Plucking at each stitch

I'll just smile as though I like
it
For in effect I do
But it's becoming unbearable
The walls beginning to bow
  Imperceptible, if my resolve she
lasts
Though this is nothing new.
But I'll just grin and carry on,

The ides have kept me hitherto.

<u>Leaves</u>

Cooling air, the senses assault
Done is the day, I've earned my
salt.
Daytime light has turned on me
On moonlit streets such trickery
The pleasant splash, those leaves
on foot
Make drunk these nostrils,
nectarous soot
Pensive mood floods the mind
And of their beauty I'm truly
blind
I do not think of Autumn whole
Only alms within my bowl
As you'll see I'm leaf inspired
Though their rudiments I have
mired
Autumn ring, the chilling tenors
Rejoiced and played in earthly
manors

That icy rush makes cold the
spirits
Yet conflagrates ye adherents
That festive smell, incense the
air!
No motive o'yours ever err
And though the day leaves more
hastily
These changing leaves get the
best o'me
Transient seconds plump and
inspir'd
Of your natural portraits I'll
never tire
The mountainside, my most
treasur'd mosaic
Whatever great works, it's more
archaic
Falling to the ground, like
listless colorful rain
Whether as the nemophilist, or
seated behind a pane

These little souls returning to
earth
Fill me with the greatest mirth
Though they exemplify an age
ended
Verbiage they have transcended
I'd fill my days with gallery
mileage
Gladly glut with their splendid
sillage
As they flit, the stuff of dreams
In their midst, pure sophrosyne.
Day or night I'm overcome
Eyes wide open and stricken dumb
Overcome with words and tune
Bursting forth, this ideal plume
And like a flower, complex in
bloom
Can't be captured, hemmed and
hewn
Vapor these words, though fall
inspire'd

No due medium, pen or lyre
Untouchable this golden essence
Wealth of ideas, gone in seconds
Appropriate, it seems to me
My head, my thoughts a leafy tree
Arrives the autumn, gold and dun
Thousands escape when I reach for
one
So I'll just watch in quiet awe
The beauty whole, no hem or haw
Not try to make that art my own
Won't reduce it to rhyme and tone
I'll simply revel their naïve
lull
Ephemeral, yes, but never dull
Shout out happily in leafy halls
Marry to words what return my
calls
Leave thou virgin, in pulchritude
pall
And question not what comes of
fall.

[Love is like Leaves]

Love is like leaves falling from
trees
The cold causes us both to fall
The heart is at ease when the
skin is pleased
Warm sheets for our survival
Icy snow falls we've given our
all
That warmth enweaved in severance
Never mind you one lasts of two
Dead branches budding petulance
But never despair be tender with
care
The leaves will fall again.

[Let this be a gift, my lover not met]

Let this be a gift, my lover not
met
This shaky sonnet of weak, boyish
hands
With eyes that gaze and trembling
mind beset
I live up the dream, stupidly
make plans
Await as your independence flits
by
Sweet introvert, we'd be a
perfect pair
Quick silver tongue, mischievous
and sly
Guilty for my presence in yours,
unfair
Your lithe little hands in my
crumby own

And cute red lips pursed with
naïveté
Pouring out poetry like pregnant
tomes
And you're wisdom abundant, be it
may
Be you different with quirk, (an
odd one, please!)
At your side, faithful I will
always be.

Bathed in Pink Light

At once reality, his matter found
Blue eyes arrested by the lighted
set
Behind those virgin pieces, cyc,
and sound
And heart's threshold, at its
suff'ring surfeit
A dazzling sun's ray of magenta
silk
Rippled, suspend, to black
cascading down
Obscured surreal faces of Love's
own ilk
Two silhouettes collude don one
pink crown
In a scene effulgent, swelling
refrain
Whole being exposed and seen from
afars
The artifice washed bare,
cleansed once again

Pretty in pink with lovely,
lovely scars
   One arm outstretched,
clasped her aura'd waist tight
   Falling like dead stars,
tears bathed in pink light

Homesick

I watched through tears
--That streamed like the one out
back
And the scattered clouds
--The ones that floated overhead
for years
A twilit ridge inurn the sun.
It was one of those rising hills
of my youth,
One my infant eyes always thought
Gave birth to the moon
Time and again.
With its innocent face smiling
That worldly crispness is lost
And the foggy past is far more
defined.
Who are these forms I've lost?
They are but phantoms,
(I tell myself)
And now intangible, those
memories

Acidic and dusted with sugar

Held suspended and taunting, like

Feet at the mouth of an open

casket.

The cold, bitter knives of

impersonal

Reunion

And rejuvenated promises

--Only now remembered, only now

forgotten—

Illuminated once again

In the dark.

Passing onward and through

--Like our time together—

Exactly like wind through these

damn dead branches

And this grave: winter-bare.

I remember the vivacity

How enlivened the sky, that I

Each day for granted took

And how so much smaller, in my

youth,

The mountains afar looked.
But there is no home,
It died when I left.
The poison I fought
Has become the blood which pumps
the heart,
Now corrupt,
Antithetical.
Nothing is more colorless, not
sky,
Nor hill, nor moon,
Or ever more formless
Than what I once called home.
Now that only exists is
deteriorated
A rotting house:
Four walls and a roof to keep
Hatred dry,
Windows and lamps, so
Hatred has eyes,
And all the people that
Hatred hates most.

How cozy it must be to sleep in
One's own bed, no?
To have some stable place,
And an ounce of certainty?
As for me, that will never be
Again.
Though the house is open,
Lock, room, and all
The home is closed forever
Without a proper epitaph.
Vain death.
Vain,
Vain,
Death.
Now all I can only turn back
And flirt with shadows
Just outside my arms
Walk with images
Shifting, growling, and oh, so
dark
--mere abstraction
--future so stark--

With no companion but defeat.
I can't hug a memory,
Nor cry on recollection's
shoulder,
Nor can my mother or sibling
consol me,
And I cry alone.
Maturation is merely widening a
distance, so
I should let them go,
Bid them adieu
Because I'll never have a home
That I can go back to.

<u>Let us</u>

Let's go away,
    To my haven in the wood
    To the lazy, little river
    Stay longer than we should
Let's watch the sun
    Lay across the leaves
    Chase it with my car
    Go until we're pleased
Let's just stand
    In some field
    Dance with the breeze
    In each other's eyes yield
Let's just forget
    The daylight will end
    Your light is my light
    So we can just pretend
Let's lay here
    In the dark, dewy lawn
    We'll go away together
    But let's stay here 'till
dawn.

Metaphor

When my hand passes along your
breast
—Your swooning tremors
translated—
Done and quiet and motionless
Our appetites full and sated.
Nothing, no passion beats
Nor does heart sing of a bond
Mere means to untied ends
Cursed, that, to never go beyond.
Laying there, as you quake with
delight
No feelings that burst
Try as I might
But, jewelry feigned and worn so
prettily
Though you are not the first.
Wander oh, Wanderer
Through fields of cut-and-dry
And ponder oh, Ponderer
What it means, her and I.

Feelings professed in autumnal
halls' rain
True Heart's contents gifted
Turned bed-pleasures again.
Is this then Love?
My mattress stained?
Is this then Love?
To entreat desires again?
My tongues are sincere,
motivating that art painted with
blood
Strained right from my heart.
But, perhaps, mine is a bad art
So prudish, so straight
Where her brushstrokes are
cherished
Not the brilliance of her paint
Perhaps, then, I'm chasing
Pure metaphor
To find Love and love
Is what Lust is for,
So, then I lay empty

With misty dreams and starry eyes
My loving hands not deferred
But outright denied.
How can we, in what sense,
In Love's definition confide?
To prove it's only a metaphor:
Not literally applied.

<u>Children Laughing</u>

A sickness, the fear

And trembling on my lips

A bearing now oh, so baffling

All these maladies seem to be

wearing

Still I hear,

To abate my scaring

Wind chimes chiming

And children laughing.

Oceans of Oceans

Tidal change and subtle movement
Fluidity of illusion.
So, like the tide
High and low
Fine arts afloat in the sea.
My commitment sails without
Metric, delineations
Lacking a logic and correctness,
Berthed, was it, into the sea
From docks in the middle of it.
How can two antitheses
--Reality, Illusion--
Be so one in the same?
Yet their paradox—their lives and
essences
Breathes a thing that dares
To laugh in the face of a
Wall.
He will know, mouth of truth,
In his mind, are follies

For at his twilight and others'
dawn
New worlds are to be born.
Dissolve, dissolve!
In the bosom of naught,
Or dip your hand to take a drink;
Water takes shape in the palm
Thick in salt and sense,
Though it flows in river, sky,
AND pond,
A tear within the ocean
To there it will return.

<u>Valley</u>

A virgin countryside
Beneath the charcoal grey,
Whose bottom is alight
Shrouds the valley,
Blanketed in snow
Still and cool and quiet.
Gentle snowflakes kiss my cheek
Sitting fireside, with hominess
Warmed at the hearth of the sky
Hushed, the world, laying asleep
From holy halls, their lullabies
Smile, do the elements,
Their dream is what has become.
And so it is,
A dream, a dream,
Though I am awake
These little souls, their
lanterns bright
Hold me to the end, across an
endless earth
White in winter's hollowness

I dream of you for all it's
worth.
Brave, must I, the whitened path
And dream of distant you—
It keeps me warm, fireside
I thank the treasures, soul
supplied.
My hearth is cold
With none to share
The brilliance of a chaste
expanse
With none to help me stare.
I have a long way to that hearth
That I'll call my own
The souls, the winter—Carry me
home!
Soon, we'll go
Your hand in mine,
Hearts akin,
Clothed embrace
We'll go, so soon
Once I've stepped from this

dream,

To have heated hearth of our own.

But now, I can't

I follow the souls' little lit

lanterns

Through the valley in the snow,

I go alone,

In their solemn palms

As they carry my lost one home.

Sleep like a Moon

The dog barks

The wind howls back

Calling the sleeping Moon

Whose slumber unnerves me

Its catatonia,

Is one I pray and hope that I

May have around me soon.

[Oh, Luna]

Oh, Luna
Carrier
Take my serenade
If this earthly love escapes
Then loving doors forbade!
Come, send my plea
Whilst I trace her constellation
And you, both hidden from mine
eyes
Trace her hand, her heart, her
eyes
To the other's harmonization
If but for one night
Pity me, or give my heart to her
The one, I know it true,
That you and I, Moon,
Both smile upon.
She whose eyes like lunar seas
So deep that hide such mystery
Whose hair enwraps my world
Like many-a brown meridian

From top to bottom with energy
From end to world's end.
Whose shadowy nature,like paradox
Alights with creamy luminescence
To outshine her companion stars
And rears my gaze Heavenward
And implores my footfall north
To cross infinity on cadence and
tune
Wishing to be where she stands
To be her sublunary perilune.
Oh, I'm mad, I'm mad
Poor, Moon my only ear
For you are not the woman
Whom I wish, this song, to hear
And yet I dream beneath the Moon
Which I hope she dreams into
That this dream
Beneath the moon
Is one she dreams of too.

<u>Be everything I want you</u>
<u>to be</u>

No, just stand there and make no
sound, be my golden girl
Let me reduce you, shh, don't
object,
For seconds be more than perfect.
Never mind your daughterhood
Or life beyond my screen
Never mind the circumstances
That made this a necessity.
You're no woman, but body parts,
I've stripped you from the
midriff down
And feasted fleshy gluttony
And removed that pesky proper
noun.
No, the eyes—Turn away!
I've forgotten your humanity
Sister, daughter, someone's mom
And erase you guiltily.

<u>Fire</u>

Hills ablaze in the western sky

Smoke, it coils through the
atmosphere

Leaving the eastern half charred
and black

Of what the twilight could not
sear.

It burns with ardor,

That western hill

The trees are tongues and burning
still

With kindling sun departing
there.

The western coals can only stare

Coming hence, a blackenedness

Whose colors echo back and forth

From ebon South

To eerie North

There it seeks to call it: "mine"

From black to purple

Blue—yellow

From there an angry Clementine

For sunk beneath the faint embers

Did go indignance of the red.

The last to go

A calming blue

It leaves so peaceful

A daylight dead.

Where have the Birds been?

An icy January
And the birds have gone.
One used to sit on a branch
And sing my mornings in.
I miss him
Like I miss my smile,
Four years, their absence
And this January has gone on a
while.
Shredded flocks
By a shredding breeze
Have moved him, the bird
To places where he's better
suited.
I still need him
I want him here,
His wings cut swathes from the
high grey clouds
And pluck me from

The icy January
Down here, resting in a hole in
the ground.
I want to fly with him, the bird
I want to be taken from here
Every fleeing bird is an
encroaching fear
That this January with become
February
And perhaps another year.
If not some escape,
Then I hope he lands outside my
window
And sings my mornings in
For I miss him
Like I miss my smile,
Five years, his absence
Wondering where he's been
And when
And if
  He'll ever come again.

Respiration or Resuscitation?

To exhale, compresses the chest
And in its place, some
chilblains,
Disgust for its being,
An annihilation
A ferocious hunger for itself,
Like the ouroboros
In every breath
Tempted by a life
For the moment gone.
To inhale
Invites it back,
A dispassionate process, no less.
The life thus stolen away
Impotent to the next breath
That I must exhale.
On this breath there comes a fear
A longing or
The urge

To lift my hands to my throat
And keep the life in my lungs
To quit exhaling
And never feel that way again.

Midnight Flowers

A little sigh, departure

From this world

To astral planes,

The cutting winds stopping their

assault

And lift tenderly

A rolling breath.

Among the stars, it disappeared

Though long before

I beat it there.

From still feet, pocketed hands

The vivid rye enwraps my palms

Whilst I, lax feet,

Walk to fields

Of the midnight flowers.

Since the sun went to its rest

Their cosmic petals unfurled

I reached up

And pinched the seeds in my right

hand

And flung them across the world.

But I could not stay,
For fear of dark
Nor force myself to leave
The upright shadows that walked
at noon
Though soon gone, pushed me away.
Caught 'tween sun and night, two
worse off half-lights
Frightened to go,
Reluctant to stay.
There I sway, I take their dower
Through this precious selenian
hour
In the forest
And over knells
To those fields
Of midnight flowers.
Their tiny halos of a velvet
white
Augur what comes: a wanting
night.
And yet their whispers,

Of dimmed succor

Show me in the yawning fields

What I came to them for:

To bathe in the pallor

That falls everywhere

And clasp my shadow's hand

To run through fields

Past the morning hours

To lose my breath

And pluck the petals

From every single midnight

flower.

Flowers in the Footpath

Light from a prism

These petal'd flo'ers grow

Breathe in weighty breaths

Versicolor whispers that quietly

follow.

They step alongside you

And spring in veneration

In the alluring prints you left

behind,

Like groves from every

indentation.

But, it's the same

Where her footfall goes

--Abreast the creekline

--In grassy seas,

--On the concrete

--In the solemn seconds that pass

by me.

I so want, ut one flower

To fill up, reserved for that one

fair.

Still, though I grab

For my partnered hand,

Thieves on breezes steal them

away

Wilting as I reach

Flowers from the footpath

And look ahead

To see the flowers

Wilting, tho' not dead.

Death would not deign to visit me

Death would not deign to visit me
Not with salute or fatal
formality
I've written letters, invitations
to dine
Perhaps to dance after some wine.
He has yet to entreat a call
I fear he may not come at all.
Given credit, I'm one apt to
hide,
I do not tread were he abides.
Occasionally,
He responds to me
In manners and way
Peculiar for this time of day
With presage cryptic, but meaning
well
That I cannot hear a personal
bell

Like that of towers

When it tolls between the hours,

That his design

(this life of mine)

Will come a calm, inaudible chime

But only in my due time.

Until he comes, for him I suffer

From his disappointments I may

grow tougher.

That, my friend, the worst of

hells

And it seems Death, from what I

tell,

Is doing his job and doing it

well.

A Pear

Has one ever known
The therapy of cutting fruit?
To pare a pear
Its skin left bare
And cleaned of its coarse green
suit?
Underneath
The white meat
Whit knife parts so easily
That in my grief
Blade unsheathed
Slice here and here and here.
Sweet relief! The nectars pour
In the sink and on the floor,
Its bloody sheen
--The loveliest I've seen!—
So I cut more and more.
I'll cut the fruit, just like I
said
One can't kill what's already
dead.

<u>These Downcast Eyes</u>

Piercing winds, fast and with
malice
Whisk away, playfully, the
revolutions,
The songs and smoky thoughts
Which I saw smoldering right in
front of me,
I see them rising in the night
At the ceiling
In dull streetlight
Mere abstractions, soft and
white,
But roar the horn
Of guilty pasts
To their image the smoke holds
fast
What soured scorn and blackened
mien
Reject my constant repentant
whine
And I travail, until I sleep

Their jeers and anger
I choose to keep.
And worthy, still I lay in bed
To even look into a dome ahead
Finite, bleak, and hopeless that
I find only appropriate.
And so close,
I grasp its bars
And wince ghosts whip and slash
At my wrists which I hold out
And tell them "harder" 'tween
teeth gnashed.
The day light comes,
And illumes my worth
By my feet spelled out in the
dirt
And just and fair, to dirt I pair
That's why my eyes
Are fixed there
All I gaze on, vibrance to ashen
waste
Ask the smoke

The he and she, I corrupted
chaste.
So my neck can take nine tails
My head is bowed in penitence
Yet, there is no flogger
But my own guilt,
My crimes, like flowers,
From proper minds wilt.
I'll keep these eyes downcast,
Where they belong
And move without progression
For I've done wrong
And with the ground I stay
To payback what debts that
vanish
To pay them everyday.

Jewel [Haiku]

A pearl from sand

Repentance, the earth murmured.

And diamond from coal.

Her broken heart

Her broken heart
Pulsed ecstatic
Her love's life drawn in twain
Her life sans fetter
Shouts, "All the better!"
Her trammels loosed again
And yet, though, the scales it
tipped
When that tragic news, it slipped
That incident
From death he leapt
Into her arms again
His accident
Her wings, it clipped
To take that heart
To Grave

[Untitled]

Broken loose and freed from a
tiring hand
One who, in restful dark,
withheld just that,
And left me to wander
To trace forms in the dark
Where troubles and trifles and
plain existence
Creep and whisper their damning
allure.
How prone am I, at this fatal
hour,
To marching idlely backwards
through
A blackened torpor
And letting exhausted candles
The haunts that hold, illume the
endless halls
That each corner and door
Some revealed appalls.
Drown their debauch which

sensually fawn

Out in the words of Byron's Don
Juan

And still feel their tempts, by
some form of folly,

That compel me to a world of
licentious melancholy.

Looking back to my bed, growing
all the number

Cursing the forces which denied
me my slumber

And what I saw in rich,
encroaching beryl

Reconciled the dreams bereft of
me:

An air of such fancy, a more
permanent scene.

A smell like the snow to the
darkness betrothed

Harkened me hence to a frosted
window pane

And out it I saw an occasion so

mundane
But at his hour, this light, the
glittering flakes effervesce,
I thought I a soul gone from this
place
And sublimed to a world
Which cannot harbor, nor ever
know, hate.
The sky was so pale which, blithe
did it shed,
So many crystalline wonders
falling from space
And resting with ease and
settling right into place
At that I saw the immaculate
ground
Uniform, sanctified, untrodden
upon,
With such power as to ward away
any notions of destiny,
And purgation of all that could
darken the mood.

Each lambent flake a seed
sprouted
'till the lawn was full of snowy
trees,
The boughs which bloomed like a
placid freeze
Themselves wearing white and all
encrusted with ice
Like holy men inept to the notion
of vice,
Reached high to the Heaven,
That which I doubt,
To catch alms on their fingers
and Gloria shout.
Miles off I hear permeating
through the calm
Respire as I arrest,
Synchronized, with time, the
lungs of the world
Until my being, minutiae, was
that of the whole
And the heart of beauty, a

natural heart,

Beat, my Confederate,

In league with my own.

In the colors of preternature,

picturesque they played

That even in my worst of lows,

My heart at that placed stayed.

The azure raiment bleached at the

wakened hour

And my eyes could not help but

look away

Blinded by some intense light

In darkness they reflect on the

previous sight

And rapture still comes in

recollection

How dull were the visions before

me lain

Their memorial no substitute, all

artifice and plain

Petty entreaties, my pinings for

that place again

Though destruction of halcyon I
durst not entertain.
Even in depression, its wiles
erotic
And at times is seizure upon me
lengthy, despotic
I've something, a snapshot, a
little dab of paint
Which even my horrors cannot
fully taint
I'll think back, I'll go back to
that very place
Which I did not wholly leave:
A place of pure bliss
Where I cannot grieve.

Poetry from the Wayside—

or: Fine

I'm not thinking of you
All the time
That's why you're (in) my poem
again
And a fleeting memory of mine.
Nothing of pith, nor something to
question:
Like a simple, transient
indigestion.
Though, you were once a wound
--Another shard of glitt'ry
ceramic—
Certainly, I'm sure, I've healed
While meditating you, the font
endemic.
Rest assured, I've loosed the
bond
Aft' some disparaged thought
Where I hit the wayside

So I no longer think of you all
the time.
...Be certain and clear,
You, gift, once so dear
That I think not of you all the
time
You that waylaid
Temper, spirit, and mind
You that effulged the soul of my
words
Of romance, of fiction
And other dribble of that kind
You, at my distance, seemed a
creature divine
From, several of my works, your
being derived.
If in life I could not have
Then in thought I shall not play
(As though thought was of any
consequence, anyway),
So, I'm happy to chime
My resistance to doting

And quitted my practices
Of ologiasing and poetic noting
And no longer think of you all
the time
Nor do I lament, nor do I whine
So, I proclaim that this is…fine
And I assure you, so am I…

"Amanda..." Trash Poetry

#1

"Amanda," she said, in a bold
assertion
"We really are the same
Person." Limp in the dew and
Wise like a sage, no wound cut
No blood shed, yet,
There was something this
Bandage shut,
Something yawning, gaping
But I don't know what...
How sad! She's crying, that
Amanda,
Shrugging 'gainst the colic rain
And almost lost in the copes-y
veranda,
Weeping softly on
Those concrete flats, wearing
"Red Tom's
And" both "Dating Matts" while

I saw her fear in that moment,
appalling, stalling
With soroitous heart, "and fear
of falling!"
Binding them tightly: "That's US
haha!"
How many laughs does a limp
spirit draw?
—(a disparaged few or none at
all…)
Still, she writes, "I am so glad"
(a huff annoyed
From Amanda, distant and sad,
that I
Can't tell why "you" ever
"joined.")
But this is not my place, a
passerby,
To pick up trash, inane and
lonely,
To cast my judgments and inquire—
why?

To heal the unbroken with words
unspoken
But scratched on refuse, she may
"[heart] you" but refuse you, too
The spirit of [heart] in Amanda
awoken
—(But she refused it, too!)
And then be a token
Some stranger takes home.

Velvet Black

Velvet black plays coy in the
breeze
Sashay 'twixt those earthen
palms, makes light
Dark corners of isolated trees.
Flitting,
The velvet, intended candid yet
so beguiles
The eyes that hide so much
And see so little
(That what they do see and don't
defile)
The ears the capture so small a
sound
Only from fingers where
machination's found
And loud to the velvet that chips
at the mortar,
Sighs at how incomplete is
disorder, to harmonize chaos

And try as I may to dismiss,
oppose,
I'm at a loss,
Locked in and froze.
Like veins in the hand and the
blood therein,
Now, only now, the velvet tells
my heart to begin,
Since, in solidity, my pulse was
rescind'd
Now, only now, may my heart
begin.
My forked tongue, it flicks, to
spit thanks to the breeze
To capture the freedom of velvety
ease, but then
As I look, in the highest of ken,
The velvet black shutters,
Then finally flees.

Fuchsia

Be not afraid, lady splashed
In the heat of our eyes:
We do not judge
Do not despise
But sit with spectator's
innocence
That hears your voice sagely and
wise—
I see you burning with
Wisdom from the single candle,
old
Filaments lighted anew, plus
The sanguinary décolletage is
somehow becoming,
Cute. The cause: it drips
Down from the head, despite it
You're doing fine; Be assured
I listen, at least,
And will not waste your time.
So speak, speak on in confidence,
withal the fuchsia face of wine

Blush now in the light of fame
Knowing you're doing just fine.

This can be read two ways

The rain of the forest

Falls through young leaves,

So sonorous, a deception.

Does it speak to a soul

Whose sun is yet risen,

And that,

Fool

Knows, nothing: whether,

It falls?

At all?

[your HEART]

...your HEART, a stump, grows,

it BREAKS, i nourish the RINGS.

See how much i LOVE...

<u>Terminus, Eros</u>

Ah, yes. I do remember—in the
annuls of the setting sun
Which gazed upon us cloister'd
couple
Just as then when this begun—
How lovely you looked to me
When I first stooped to take your
hand:
The air was pink from rushing
blossoms
Blown as though caught where
waves meet sand
Out o'er the horizon's sea
Of lapis stones and perfect
lilies,
Our marble vessel stood calm
afloat
As Time she ceased her constant
chatter
Our love, on eternity, she thusly
wrote.

2.

A promise kept where we abide
I see the spell on you ascribed
As though not a minute since then
had died
Our eyes are locked
As is my reverence
Wedded in both hand and Time
Union'd there upon the hill
One constant spirit, forever
'twine
My hand in yours,
Your eyes in mine
And all the day a vernal eve.

3.

Forever faithful, 'till we're
parting dust
N'er a band, nor jem's allure
Compel me from this meeting just
And we're betrothed
As one amorous, fixed stone
You're my bride of marble pure

I, your husband, and yours alone.

4.
The snow must fall, but never
does
Nor do hands of some final hour
The face of parting averts his
glower,
And no such sadness entreats us
here,
You only cry the tears of rain,
In concert so do I,
Even our sentiments commune where
they ought,
And strain, does not
Our open home, where the live
rest peaceful:
Espoused to none but plots and
vine
Widowed from both bride and Time,
Pining for that permanence, the
comfort of our kind.

For they the living, asleep and buried,
Rejoice at such, our fates prolonged,
For what it is: the stuff of dreams.
From thence, 'till now, it tarried
And, just as then, you beam.
        5.
Your blankened eyes are filled with me,
Not soiled by another sight
Beneath this alter of pallid stone
All I see is placid white:
My eyes filled with thee.
Many a-year may have passed
But we're indifferent to present, future, past
And though our company is but the dead

They can watch us

Forever, watch us wed.

     6.

That august sun, such reverie

Upon it portents I could read

A neverending waxen love

Into that permanence of history

wove

That could proclaim, our

sentiments same,

Into pink winds, through homes of

the dead

The fused seasons through which

we tread

Dismissing the failings of human

emotion,

Embosoming a steady climb,

Thus envisaging the statue's

notion

That Eros decreed so few would

find

Love protected by Terminus

Its constellation we cusp.

     7.

That craft'd on love,

transcending this

Oceans of present, future, past

Our ship it sails on maxim, not

mast,

A message to all the staring

world:

Only a love like ours may last.

<u>Hometown</u>

I saw myself walk up to my native
door, a vagrant
To familiar plots, concrete slabs
of home town lots
Leveled and full of houses,
That grew with me and with the
weeds
That persist and grow without me.

Returning here is to turn back
time
While the sun still sets,
And collects regrets in the
stagnant pools
In my little stream that no
matter where I choose to walk
Flows on past me, forever a
stranger.

The pining air in my childhood
park

Blows against me, my foreign
hair; against the grain
Its course and form
Ushers in the summer that refuses
to warm
And stifles sobs, the tears in
their own ice.
In these alley ways, the school
house and country store
Idylls of Rustica my young days
chose to ignore
Where, there, open arms were
still open
To deplore
I'm a louse here, and nothing
more,
To these old walking paths: now
new puzzles and mazes.
Nestled in my native strath, the
town pastoral
Blinks in the sleeping sky while
I walk asking it for room again,

Deafs its ear 'till and dusk
calls back "Itinerant!"

My feet may shuffle, but I still
see home;
The very place is still mine
At least by the paint on its
welcoming sign…
But that time has passed, so too
the time for crying
Or lying that familiar plots are
thrones to be reclaimed,
Old loves, half-done, still open
for redemption, as though
We're both enveloped underneath
the very same sun,
And forgiveness, now, comes
As easily as it came…

Dust settles, quite like the
dusk, all across the cusp of town

My well-known antique a very
clear half-image
Seen as a still, running in the
split-wood fences
Real, like a movie:
A penny show through glasses
without lenses;
The town's night is bathed in
rosy recollection,
Mine is bleak, made bleaker
looking back while leaving
It soaked in the light of home
diminished
Leaving every goddamn thing
Feeling unfinished.

[untitled]

Go, as the river runs, this thing
Flung miles in the silver sky,
This little thing of imagination
And my feet are still;
Glass fogs with phantoms' finger
prints.
Coffee and tea are my adventure,
The dead revel in their histories
and fantasies;
What shore has my soul touched on
now?
High lofts from where I stand:
The mileful ocean of baseless
sand
Taunting echo from the gulls
Sets the navigator in me to
swelling
But in domestic walls,
Safety reconciles this, all this
order
Seems amiss, I cannot tell

For the life of me
If the sky is the color of ghosts
Or spirits.

<u>Indignation</u>

Sulphurous clouds torn and rent
By the wicked
Fingers, boiling hydrogen
In its arching bent grin
Pale pink and ravaging
contentment.
Spectators lift their gazes,
acolytes,
Like alms heavenward till wild
cracks
Break the shifting firmament
And Heaven falls into their
palms.

Chaos Theory

He and I stood abreast

Near the grinding smell of rail

and screaming metal

Teetering on the tresses,

Between what seemed

A wordless fear—I touched the

Absurd

Felt it thunder at my fingers

Great iron backs carried great

iron

Caskets spelled with

chrysanthemums, those words

As spit, came from our tongues.

Each one, he knew

Would fall as rain, where I saw

the damn thing

Derailing, and both plunged our

hands

Ahead, and then

It did: it fell, inuring, I died

And he was killed, the vultures
spied,
The wind brought my hands, his
touched
To see the end,
A sea,a channel of casualties
When he stepped and gossiped on
And I floated meaninglessly,
thinking
This is sublimation in the 21st
century.

<u>Ants</u>

Whit-ringed red
Black-ringed white
Aluminum hearts, plastic ants
Angered, but do they know it?
Midst their congestion,
One narrative
Bleeds out exhaust, and then
another, and then more
Begging for a voice
To tell them, but the words
Are forever lost,
Bed-time stories will be told
In new lines
Promising something gilded
Or maybe just jaded—
Whatever, it's all the same
beauty.

Mere Rite of Passage

Those ceremonies that once seemed
for me
Now thundering in song elsewhere
As in generations before:
Note, meter, and unaltered time
Just as in generations before,
The music passed without one
thought more:
One torch lit another.
Out burnt hands that carried them
Still red and throbbing
For Autumn's flame
Still grasping for a bygone day
Where we may light another
And be the hero
Now we thought we were
Not fear the darkness now,
cowering
For wicks could not inure
Cataclysm of our own evenings:
The coming of our longest night,

Starless with the keenest blank
Fraught with equanimity and
cooling, pleasant weather,
Still grasping for the bygone day
Where one torch lit another.

A burial

"Travesty," those orange words
spilled across the highway lines
Came on swathes of a stilled
And perfect evening time,
'Tween buffeting air and
screaming music
It seems but a step in a cyclic
progression,
Or the lines that commence
This processional of cars
That follows, to the site, trails
of incense,
Tears of mourn and memoirs.
Towards the hills canvassed in
reluctant ennui
Jutting in the shadows the
bleached ribs and pearly jaw
lines
That, at times, may have looked
alive, yet now

They rest static as the dead
ought to be.
I sense I'm getting close, the
organ surges its triumph
As it does the sanctuary,
My head swells with deep booming
sound,
The lyric of the preacher without
need to expound,
Too late as the organ shan't stop
or abate
As I pass through churchyard
admonished "Hell,
Is truth realized only too late."
Though I am soothed by that song
of my youth,
Lyric'd by many-a familiar
cadence and tune
Vestiges of naïveté play on the
lips
But, "Hell is truth only realized
too soon."

I wait at its back and reminisce
The coming great years were
something to fight for
With life, defend,
But I now see that I spent those
last seconds
Waiting for them to end,
Whilst prayers of hollow wind
abound
Escaped to show something holds
on, at least
Pretends,
Will remain after me, aft' I've
settled in the ground,
To be as a sunset and come back
around.
I feel like a sun, burning in
fury,
Not simply a shimmer in the
vastness afar,
Or the muddy face of fetid puddle
Simply rippling like a star.

Keep driving! Don't cease my tiny
hearse!
Just now do I hear the mourners'
verse,
It sounds so golden and couldn't
get worse!
But the organ has ceased,
The daylight, it rots
(Never mind that, I'll charge it
with haught!)
And the processional laughs as
they go to their plots
Their verses fall too coward to
brave
The ice and the snow that is to
come, mine fall stricken
With every sense of the word
'dumb,'
But the sun reassuring with it
warmth-giving rays
Will be sure to put flowers next
to our graves.

Driving

A balmy air plumes in the valley
Two giants'; backs flank
Bearing what feels a pittance
(the weight of the world is
nothing
Compared to something in tatters)
To me.
Though the groves incense
With honey, the streams
Feeding an easel of vernal pair
I only know it along the
serpentine twist of the macadam
Writhing its way to destruction
From there;
I would turn if the road would
end.
So few souls 'tween the shade and
beam
A place where the mind sets to
dream with force
And only that

For that I turn when I reach the
end,
Uphold purest meaning of course,
Perhaps then, a pittance, this
burden will seem
The mile markers, Olympian
As I reach their end, to see
Belief in this balm is merely to
pretend,
But the country wind is sweet
Sweet and belying,
To ascend, to ascend
The pinnacle keeps sighing, to
wake from a dream is merely
To die
Yet, it is only a dream
And worth only that.

Idler

The very sky fell to greet a
wandering shade
Only by a falling light
His form and frame were made
Calling, with his silence
A Solsticine, on whom
None could find reliance.
What of this world walked with
the fog
But he, small,
In mist, walks without his giant
At the fields of Arcad'
To golden plains
A Dasein, in which nothing is
flawed
Standing at media
Fit for the amused, too tall to
walk
On and on, on shoulders the sun
takes its leave
Its rest.

To giants the day is drudgery,
when one dawn falls
And moon, I, dreading it won't
find me
My idler goes in wistful mists
On to the breaking light
Onward to the reddened night
My idler goes in wistful mists
Silent, absolutely.

Blade of Regret

There is a wound that sits behind
the eye
Triad tonality, a fearsome sigh
Plucks a bloody chord
Lyric'd by the word "why?"
Acid fingers grin in lust
Anticipating another thrust into
the belly
Of time gone by
Hot skin taut and merely waiting
For suicides to release their
hands
In the chain their concert makes
Eternities in some hellish waste
lived in only seconds.
How strong the forces are!
So steep a severing blow!
Still fresh a carrion scar,
festering miles still to go
To beset the pinkest eves
This blade of regret

Within a greater narrative,
Tiny little vignettes
Armed in fashion of drunken odes
Those promises sworn to keep
Accompanied by such pathos woes
Accoutered, finally, in weep.
Brandished when it's not so
fresh:
This minor paring of my flesh
Gleaming in the summer laughs
To caterwaul my gaff, or plural
if you like
The humor undercuts enormity
Or screams on shafts in biting
breezes
This lived-in clime
I, this prey, displeases.
Unsheathed, the memories, in
jovial acts of war
Besiege, beleaguer, the since-
immured

True blood and guts long-since
obscured
By friendliness, camaraderie
Intentions jester-pure
Trick suppressing-shields raised,
jaundiced wills will not deflect
No blade or arrow of regret.

<u>Aeviternus</u>

Deep beneath a pillowed sky,
there
A restful restlessness abides
Nestled in a perennial hill
Whose sentinel trees raised their
hands,
White with subtle deference,
They do not usher the world
flowing 'hind,
But show me an islet high above
time.
I sat there in ponderance at the
stagnation of clouds
Holding on one end a gold string
of a kite
My thoughts tethered to those
ghosts,
Those wights, sitting amongst me,
those by-gone eras
And down, on me, some vague
horror weighted

To them it was the Stones that
made them feel dated
I thought I could feel slippage,
some loss of traction
They? They bore a whole lifetime
without
Satisfaction.
The breeze smells of gossip and
Jaeger on their lips;
Everything is on point: dances,
romances, localist quips.
Whoever would have guessed
Memories ablur could be the most
vivid?
Such, I suppose, is an art form
insipid.
I had to step away from this
field of time
It had overtaken, that shadow of
mine
All the trees now, bow and they
bend

Prostrate, like a weeping willow.
When they step out into the
world,
A bath of gold in the dusk of
their lives
Shall fall before their feet,
denude from their shadows
To run on ahead.

[untitled]

I thought at once the hands

Took hold of life

But only to loosen them

Inside the pockets:

It merely seems a bit tight

today.

<u>Professional Liar</u>

Who are these people?

Eyes seems to say that, despite their

Aversion,

Come my way, anyway,

Angered, annoyed, knowing my game

When I can only keep calm

Play it coy

Then hook with a pitch I'd been working on

The night before,

Fish in a bowl that would rather run and lie

With something half baked

Thinking me a snarling force

Eyes, wings, and teeth and all.

I've got expenses! And bills to pay, too!

We're not so different: me and you!

I like you and want to know you

Not fleece you out of money

—that would make a good paycheck,

though—

The only thing is that I am a

liar,

But the most honest you'll ever

find,

No meatless notions

Of pithy truths, a goodness

inherent

And malisms abound for good sense

to defeat.

I won't lie and tell you

I'm doing good deeds

But I won't hide behind that veil

That paints evil on me,

Because it's not true, because it

won't hold

It's merely the atoms there in

the fold

The lines that represent the

dichotomy

Are all grey
Too grey for the eyes to see,
And so much easier is it to look
at the blurred crispness
Of righteousness
To brandish a sword spilling with
light
And holy fire
Than to accept I've got a job,
I breathe your same air
And if I could choose I'd rather
not be there.
But that's my only way to survive
in your world
My time a thing of commerce
Shaped up and lip curled
And atrocities like me occur
everyday
Requisite a bachelor's
And with a higher in pay,
Kind of like the one you work
8 hours a day.

[untitled]

Does she believe in a half-built
home?
Or its hole in the ground?
I've taken the roam
A wide roof I claim to my own
And how much I miss the walls
The studs that creak and waver
To savor the freedom of the
breeze.
Life plays on the palm fronds
Not much hope can hang on either.

[untitled]

Everlasting art

Her mind is the rose window

Dust, is her body

[untitled]

You are no item to me,
But a specter who winds through
the bones
Elusive, frightening
Warm and whitening in a cemetery
yard
You've returned for a purpose
That is not my own.
My eulogy goes as thus on a
stone, waiting
Conjuring a spirited hand and
knowing
Earthly words cannot tempt
A soul who rejected Heaven.

Simply Un-moving

Never has the image of a sweet

old woman

Repulsed me,

As one in front of a TV.

Don't ask me why,

I do not know

Something about stasis

And a wasted will

Comes off as virulent.

On not thinking Broke

I can feel it:
Public discourse, social love
Coming on in the summer,
The salaries of the highest above
Can heal endless fissures,
Lift away the yoke,
Shift away the thinking mind
From thinking of it broke,
And have them go to work.
Simply said and done.

Pinned against a Wall(mart): Taker's Philosophy and its Students

Two-daughters succession go
astride
One hunched in apathy
The other in defeat
I could have seen beauty in
progeny
Before it was
Crushed
By artificial gravity
Smelling of blood-stained
pittances
And a taker's philosophy,
Their lunch-box notions
And plastic dreams
Rattled the bars on a shopping
cart.
Do they, I wonder,

Feel their ease at pain? Or

luxury, woe?

Though their smiling faces

Were promised, now reach

To Paradise,

I can seem them

Crushed

Beneath them, too:

Updated, upgraded, brand-spanking

new

All they ever hoped to be,

Customized

Head-to-fucking-toe.

<u>Why Would I?—A Different Kind of Love (poem)</u>

I could take your hand
        But then I would restrain you.
                And why would I want to
do that?
You're so perfect you should be free.
I could draw hearts on your skin
        But then it'd be as though you branded mine
                And why would I want to
do that?
        You're beautiful even without me there.
I could swim through your veins, dance in your eyes
        But then I'd be trapped and invisible to you

And why would I want to
do that?

You're too special to waste
from on the inside.
I could have you like in
consummation,

But then we'd have ruined
all that could be

And why would I want to
do that?

You're worth too much to
just take and not give.
I could tell you I love you

But then you're placed
second to me

And why would I want to
do that?

You're always going to
finished tied with me
I could marry you and clasp your
hands in rings

But then you'd be, by
statute, legally mine
            And why would I want to
do that?
      You're not the zoo animal
destined to wilt.
Why make us apart-of when we're
grand wholes alone
Neither are we halves-of or the
other's-better
When we could be two, with lives
of our own,
Standing, by divided love, beside
and together.

[untitled]

So it is I who has invented this
world
That glows in a balmy way
Phosphorescent on the breeze
Of youth,
Crystalline by the snow
Of age,
Acrid, by the ill
Of man?
I don't remember being born
In an arena, one babe in a brood
of sharks.
Yet, I invented it? I welcomed
All the hatred, in general,
An enormous enormity?
It goes, I guess, without saying,
I must project these envisionings
Since I've done nothing to stop
it.

<u>Lushness in borrowed</u>

<u>garden</u>

One plough amongst many runs
'cross
An infertile campus
The threat of first frost
Following in her tow
To reap one something
From the settled bed of salt.
Combing seeds in the sod,
The anchor in her womb
Drags—soon, so soon,
The distance won't widen, the
burden will stop
Her knees will buckle in debt and
chance
Will lock her where she falls
Her failure will sprout and
flower.
The falling sweat flashed years
before

To the juice beading in single
drops
A vain nectar of her other's
field,
Biding her, come, eat of
appearance;
Her crop was brown, but budding,
She left her crop to die.
Unprepared for the neglected
miles
She toiled in the changing leaves
And, of course, the gilded fellow
Him, the established man
Could draw her in: with gleaming
ivies
Red, tight, yellow, sweet
A wine of the eyes that sits on
the vine
Families of prodigality smiles
with brimming bags
Baskets pregnant in promise,

Those happy mouths full of praise
and food.
For there, she followed
That procession, honest, in the
borrowed garden.

Exploration of the Grey

All the worst things in life
Start with a:
A-social
A-theist
A-sexual.
A-bominations to be corrected,
but,
And although, in the hands of a
body
The blame must go
Tight-gripped and freely clasped
A smile hangs like a necklace.
For, they ask, what grows,
On what shore that glance a
thirsting road
Where no artisan of wells
Lets run his craft
Burst with life?
What vines may couple, transect
dead veins
Still in a bed of salt

But dead and grey shades of the
true?
None,
It would seem, can carry the
sweet
Of fertile seeds along the
water's edge
It is but passing as its
plumpness
Withers and drops
Apart, epistle, a dogma.
This vampiric little heart takes
no form
In Narcissus' pool it does not
Glisten in the waters calm
Despite the furious mouth
And, gone, lost of all that made
it whole.
I go back to the source of the
Grey valley flume
Unknown to impetus,

Cannot find its way in the
endless roads
And paths in the sun-baked skin,
The wind may blow salt in my eyes
though
The music of its basin fills my
ears:
Waves breaking and pressing
On soft earthen lines, scrap-book
memories
Faded at the edges like Polaroids
Unfold from the waves of purity
In the sand of an empty shore.
I peer idly into the glimmering
stream
No red heart beating,
But a grey heart; one simply
searching, pining
For a grey love to begin
And the world that I know
They belong in.

Bottle

To travel and live on a roaring
ocean
A life of ebbing and flowing
waves
And transformation
Is seductive to my
Ink-stained fingers
Begging to wash in the surf
To ready themselves for some
journey
Ahead.
Prepare the vessel!
Call here the mark!
But only a few tick before we
finally
Embark; the orange arch of salt-
spray and freedom
Wade in the glass of the inert
sea
Directed in the way of time's
linearity

Perhaps to a coast on only one
design:
A message in a bottle
To wherever the wind calls mine
With but a simple story
For whomever it may find.

This is the new day?

I can look forward to the coming
day
At the hum of the speakers'
mournful twang
The strings—too many hours
To go
Till the top of the next one
When the new day begins
When a real dawn
Meets my eye
When a real sun
May shine.
The hands are jammed though
And hidden between, a soft and
empty prayer,
Bounces between their contrite
arms—
Where will it go when they close?
Where will it go when they open?
Amen: the futile-day
Begins.

[haiku]

If over the tear

Called back to the lonely eye

It would be too late

[haiku]

Parallax, soft limbs

Weave the souls' hearts, water
skin

The wine that love brought.

Never—A promise

Come, ode-to-be,

Never let my get so close

That I should turn to graphite

That which set notes

To a discordant symphony,

Lyrics to that beautiful

muteness.

Never—I promise—will you be my

poem

You've mastered an art

Only dreams could capture

Half as well.

You make me seek and chase

A fantasy

And long to capture what, before

I never thought.

I am left in division:

Do I love what I can't have?

If so, how?

Do I release what eschews chains,

Arrests me having done the
better?
O, then this I hear a locket
Whole, in faith, on my breast
And lest I'm to sail
Towards an in an eastern destiny
The key will blow in warm
From the west
Strangely, a pattern unlike my
own
On wings that flutter
Free
And I will, somehow, hold the key
That, somehow, predates
Her western destiny.
Two lockets broken
And chains entwined
Shall render useless an eager
hand
But still the palsy that urges it
Amidst the ailing hate of it:
Love in its purest.

Alief, conviction,
Separates wind from certain
Doom, hate of love: conflict.

[untitled]

The sun does arise

In that aubade way

It spills out over petals

Infinitely

So silent but a discourse:

A camp of brook and pale-freckled

Leaves,

A clamor of engines

Escaping the scene

Too busy, too distant

To actualize their hum.

At the intercession of wood and

modern man

I stood dutiful, tenuous,

Apt to standing still

'Tween what has my calling

And what, my will:

This aesthetic simplicity,

resplendent awe

Stays with the punch-card

On my way to work

But I know I'll stand at the edge
Once more.

Lamp-lit

...How ironic:

The lampshade sits in darkness

Illuminating nothing

Wondering nothing

No little spark to unrest the

prevailing.

I see there, a faith

Without foundation

 A singularity of affection.

But something blooms forth

An un-amazed belief,

A fact as it should—it pops

To life—

Nothing more of the dark

But tight walls

And clutter.

An echo keeps saying,

Don't waste life on trying to

live

But living in spite of

The life that you give...

Eclectia

Long, reaches a grasping valley
Contracts a grimace shared by
tenets:
Close-door plumage and lock-key
breezes
Approach of determined skepticism
A judged eye comes avowed,
This pirouette of garbage
On it mere scratches can be
found.
Noisily, this presage our perfect
clouds
Bemoan a devil so quick to drone—
The futile-fly—will he make it?—
Only speaking in snapshots.
Such shutterings run the mileage
old
Darken the edifice, all be told,
For the dawning wash furies only
in bits

Foeish stutterings 'tween doors
can only persist
In drawing power from raw, the
imperfect
And trash that elemented it.
Spoken true, it ate the fame
Broken glasses cracked away
We never saw storms quite the
same.

End

Check out my other poetry at:

http://hellopoetry.com/jp-goss

Check out my blog at:

http://jpgossauthor.wordpress.com
/

www.ingramcontent.com/pod-product-compliance
Lightning Source LLC
La Vergne TN
LVHW051122080426
835510LV00018B/2194